Nathan Levy & Adam Laningham's

Quotes To Keep You Brilliant

Quotes from

Nathan Levy, Leon Kaatz, Peter Bakker, and many other well-known, and less well-known thinkers

Quotes Gathered by

Nathan Levy and Adam C. Laningham

NATHAN LEVY BOOKS, LLC

18 MOORLAND BOULEVARD

MONROE TWP, NJ 08831

Phone- 732 605-1643 Fax-732-656-7822

nlevy103@comcast.net

Cover Art by Adam C. Laningham

Thank you to:

Peter Bakker and Leon Kaatz for your amazing quotes, inspiration, and friendship over the years.

Candy Justicia for your contributions to this book. We wish you well on your travels!

Dominique Zuani-Levy, Amstrong Laningham, & Tammy Turcott for your support over the years and helping to edit this book with us.

Introduction

When author/collector Leon Kaatz shares his wisdom with his family, friends, and followers, these are his first words; "gifts come in all shapes, sizes and colors. Some are practical, some are fun, and some get exchanged. There are few gifts one can give that are better than the wisdom learned in one's lifetime. I hope you will welcome some of what I have learned, use what suits you, and be a better person for the experience. Please add your own wisdom. As you increase your bank of wisdom, share it generously with those who are important to you. It is truly the gift that keeps on giving."

WE AGREE!

We have added numerous quotes from Nathan's mentor (Peter Bakker) and Nathan's own collection from his workshops, training and guest appearances to our book as well as other great sayings from family members, friends, and more famous or infamous characters.

Adam Laningham and Nathan Levy also add advice on the following pages for teachers and parents on practical ways to use dynamic quotes when teaching, parenting, or in just enjoying daily life.

Enjoy!

What to Know

Quotes and proverbs are often shortcuts to high level thoughts. More importantly, they start and/or stop great actions in people. The old single quote "Make haste not waste," has served to slow me down when needed on many occasions. We have created one compendium of quotes to provide readers with many wise thoughts in capsules to bring joy and wisdom to our readers for sharing and reflection.

For those of you who teach, these are tools to summarize lessons, help learners see bigger ideas, and bring joyous learning that might have you making lifetime impact 20-30 years later.

For those of you in business or politics you will find tools to liven and shorten the important messages you plan to deliver.

For entertainers and speakers, you can shorten your oratory and broaden your messages at the same time.

We love great quotes. Please enjoy our collection and make yourself smarter.

Nathan Levy, Author/Educator

A word from Master Educator Adam Laningham author of Gifted Children and How Trauma Impacts Them.

How to Use Quotes to Engage Learners

Having been in education for over 20 years, I have learned that quotes are a simple, but effective, tool a teacher can use to increase student learning. Because quotes can be viewed in infinite ways, using them encourages creativity, engagement through discussions, and a student's critical thinking skills. I have seen and used the power of quotes to enhance the learning of my students in many grade levels and at multiple schools.

Some ways to use quotes in your classroom or at home with your children are:

Novelty - Get Kid's Attention!

Students, especially gifted students, love novelty. Anything a teacher or parent educator can do to mix it up a bit can help to keep their students interested and enjoy learning is incredibly valuable. Quotes are a wonderful, yet simple way to get children's attention.

Quotes can be silly, odd, perplexing, meaningful or simple and ordinary. They are a little different each time and it keeps kids guessing. When you have discussions over quotes you never really know where it will lead, and that is part of the fun… Fun for both the students and the teacher! Keeping joy in the learning process cannot be overestimated.

Engagement - Keep Kids Thinking!

The activities and discussions you can do with quotes are a powerful tool to keep students engaged in the learning. Quotes allow for multiple interpretations when they are discussed, you never really know where the discussion will go. Students should be encouraged to share their thoughts, explain their thinking (which includes their viewpoints and background knowledge), listen to others, and justify their thoughts and ideas.

A well facilitated discussion encourages active listening skills and the appreciation for all views to be expressed. If a teacher has an open and welcoming environment, students will want to share and contribute to the discussion. This involvement helps to keep them wanting to listen, contribute, and think. The structure of the discussions may need to be more structured at first, but as students begin to accept and meet the participation expectations, you can open up and be more relaxed and less structured.

Thinking Skills - Increase Kid's Critical Thinking Skills!

Children, even gifted children, need to be taught how to think and solve problems. There are many activities and resources available to this end, but discussions based on quotes are simple and effective. Being able to use their background knowledge, multiple thinking skills, and knowledge gained from others to help solve problems is a valuable life skill for our children to be able to master. Thinking critically to analyze a problem and using collaboration skills will be used in any future educational path and almost any career field. Starting simple tasks and discussions around quotes is an easy way to start this thinking process.

Introduce Units or Lessons - Start Kid's Thinking!

In addition to the discussions, quotes are great writing prompts. A response to a quote is a simple fast writing activity. These are great to start off a class or for a transition to a new activity. Encouraging students to do frequent, quick writing responses is important to help organize their thinking and prepare them for longer writing tasks. Many times, just starting your thoughts to a prompt hangs students up in the writing process. Frequently going through this task is a great benefit to many students.

Quotes to start a unit of study are a great tool to get students thinking. Picking a quote that ties into the unit like a scientific thinker, historical figure, a reaction to an event, etc. can help set the direction for the unit. For these, you would want to thoughtfully select the quote to direct the thinking.

You may want to share the background of the author or quote itself, after students have shared their thoughts or, better yet, wait until the conclusion of the unit. Waiting until the conclusion of the unit allows students to keep wondering and trying to make the connections. It is always fun to see when, in the unit, the author of the quote is brought in, to see how the students react. Many will naturally start talking about it. Many may now want to change their views based on what is learned.

A quote can be a simple yet effective way to start a unit and keep students thinking.

Get even smarter, read these quotes!

I would rather be accused of honest arrogance than hypocritical humility.

- *Frank Lloyd Wright*

No one suffers the way one does on a mountain simply for a beautiful view. A summit isn't just a place on a mountain. It is a tiny scrap of a dream made real; indisputable proof that our lives have meaning.

- *Ron Dietzman*

Never let fear of failure stop you from trying.

- *Leon Kaatz*

When I was 17, I thought my father was the dumbest man in the world. When I was 25, I was amazed at how much he had learned.

- *Mark Twain*

What is it to be a gentleman? The first to thank and the last to complain.

- *Serbian proverb*

Show me a man who cannot bother to do the little things and I will show you a man who cannot be trusted to do the big things.

- *Lawrence D. Bell*

Learn as if you were going to live forever. Live as if you were going to die tomorrow.

- *Mahatma Gandhi*

Love is purely a creation of the human imagination . . . the most important example of how the imagination continually outruns the creature it inhabits.

- *Katherine Anne Porter*

I'm a realist and so I think regretting is a useless occupation. You help no one with it. But you can't live without illusions even if you must fight for them, such as 'love conquers all'. It isn't true, but I would like it to be.

- *Marlene Dietrich*

I haven't been everywhere, but it's on my list.

- *Susan Sonta*

Nothing annoys a man as to hear a woman promising to love him 'forever' when he merely wanted her to love him for a few weeks.

- *Helen Rowland*

Here is to lost loves; and here is to loves who moved suddenly and left no forwarding address.

- *Cosmo Fishhawk and Shoe*

It's a rare man who knows which of his lovers it would be wisest to marry. It's a rare woman who doesn't.

- *Marilyn Vos Savant*

What counts in life is not the mere fact that we have lived. It is what difference we have made to the lives of others.

- *Nelson Mandela*

Don't be scared of what excites you. Always stay curious about yourself and the people and places around you. Focus on the work and goals you have set for yourself, and never compare yourself to others.
- *Ingi Mehus*

Keep working.
- *Katherine Owens*

Everything a woman does, she must do twice as good as a man. Fortunately, that is not difficult.
- *Patty Antinerel*

A mother never realizes that her children are no longer children.

- *Holbrook Jackson*

"I never met a client that I didn't like."

- *Will Rodgers*

Will Rodgers never met some of my clients.

- *Leon Kaatz*

If you really want to get somewhere, put your eyes on that horizon. Dream a little. Set a goal that is romantic but reasonably possible, then set out to achieve it.

- *B.C. Forbes*

If in the last few years, you haven't discarded a major opinion or acquired a new one, check your pulse, you may be dead.

- *Gelett Burgess*

I spent my whole life searching until I found the perfect woman. Alas, it turned out she was searching for the perfect man.

- *Unknown*

You cannot change those around you, but you can change those who are around you.

- *Unknown*

I believe the art of living consists not so much in complicating simple things as in simplifying things that are not.

- *François Hertel*

I think, therefore I am.

- *Rene Descartes*

We may hold different points of view, but it is in times of stress and difficulty that we most need to remember that we have much more in common than there is dividing us.

- *Queen Elizabeth II*

If you only associate with people who think the same way you do you substantially limit your opportunities to learn.

- *Leon Kaatz*

Give all men your ear but few your tongue.

- *William Shakespeare*

Simplicity is making the journey of this life with just enough baggage.

- *Charles Dudley Warner*

Success isn't about the end result, it's about what you learn along the way.

- *Vera Wang*

Excess on occasion is exhilarating. It prevents moderation from acquiring the deadening effect of habit.

- *W. Somerset Maugham*

Blessed are they who can laugh at themselves for they shall never cease to be amused.

- *Unknown*

The ills of today must not cloud the horizons of tomorrow.

- *William J. Mayo*

The difference between an autobiography and an unauthorized biography is like the difference between an account of your life written by your mother and one written by your mother-in-law.

- *Marilyn Vos Savant*

The choices we make dictate the lives we lead.

- *Bill Rago*

My son is my son 'til he takes him a wife; but my daughter is my daughter for the rest of her life.

- *Jewish Proverb*

How we spend our days is, of course, how we spend our lives.

- Anne Dillard

If love were an animal, what species would it be and could you train it? Love would be two animals: a hummingbird and a snake. Both are perfectly untrainable."

- *Cheryl Strayed*

The most valuable of all talents is that of never using two words when one will do.

- Thomas Jefferson

It is the duty of the press to comfort the afflicted and to afflict the comfortable.

- *H.L. Mencken*

If you can spend a perfectly useless afternoon in a perfectly useless manner, you have learned how to live.

- *Lin Yutang*

Take into account that great love and great achievement involve great risk.

- *Dalai Lama*

He does not seem to me to be a free man who does not sometimes do nothing.

- *Cicero*

Nothing in the world will take the place of persistence. Talent will not; nothing is more common than unsuccessful men with talent. Genius will not; unrewarded genius is almost a proverb. Education will not; the world is full of educated derelicts. Persistence and determination alone are omnipotent. The slogan "Press on" has solved and always will solve the problems of the human race.

- *Calvin Coolidge*

If I had my life to live over, I would start barefoot earlier in the spring and stay that way later in the fall. I would go to more dances. I would ride more merry-go-rounds. I would pick more daisies.

- *Nadine Stair*

I am not for myself, who will be for me? But if I am only for myself, what am I?

- *Talmud*

Capitalistic competition brings out the best in products and the worst in man.

- *The Wall Street Journal*

Don't surrender all your joy for an idea you used to have about yourself that isn't true anymore.

- *Cheryl Strayed*

Whatever you do, do it with passion. The rest comes by itself.

- *Fabiola Haro*

A holiday gives one a chance to look backward and forward, to reset oneself by an inner compass.

- *May Sarton*

The time to relax is when you don't have time for it.

- *Sydney J. Harris*

They also serve who only stand and wait.

- *John Donne*

A single seed can turn into a forest. A single heart can transform a nation.

- *Bryan Thao Worra*

A vacation is having nothing to do and all day to do it in.

- *Robert Orben*

No man stands taller than he who stoops to help a fallen comrade.

- *Unknown*

Making predictions is always difficult, particularly if it is about the future.

- *Yogi Berra*

The best way to get most husbands to do something is to suggest that perhaps they are too old to do it.

- *Ann Bancroft*

The discovery of a new dish does more for human happiness than the discovery of a star.

- *Anthelme Brillat-Savarin*

To be yourself in a world that is constantly trying to make you something else is the greatest accomplishment.

- *Ralph Waldo Emerson*

Keep your eyes wide open before marriage, half shut afterwards.

- *Benjamin Franklin*

There is no love sincerer than the love of food.

- *Bernard Shaw*

I married Miss Right. I didn't know her first name was Always.

- *Henny Youngman*

If there is no struggle, there is no progress.

- *Frederick Douglass*

Those who ignore history are doomed to repeat it.

- *George Santayana*

Good judgment comes from experience, and a lot of that comes from bad judgment.

- *Will Rogers*

There is only one difference between a long life and a good dinner; that, in the dinner, the sweet comes last.

- *Robert Louis Stevenson*

Everybody needs a passion. That's what keeps life interesting. If you live without passion, you can go through life without leaving any footprints.

- *Betty White*

The art of living is more like wrestling than dancing.

- *Marcus Aurelius*

Good manners will open doors that the best education cannot.

- *Clarence Thomas*

The real voyage of discovery consists not in seeing new landscapes, but in having new eyes.

- *Marcel Proust*

If there were no bad people there would be no good lawyers.

-   *Charles Dickens*

It does no good to have a lot of irons in the fire if the pilot light is out.

-   *Leon Kaatz*

The second happiest day in a boat owner's life is the day he buys his boat. The happiest day in his life is the day he sells it.

-   *Unknown*

The time to make friends is before you need them.

- *Peter Bakker*

Hope is the thing with feathers that perches in the soul, and sings the tune without the words, and never stops at all.

- *Emily Dickinson*

A minority group has "arrived" only when it has the right to produce some fools and scoundrels without the entire group paying for it.

- *Carl T. Rowan*

Success without honor is an unseasoned dish; it will satisfy your hunger, but it won't taste good.

- *Joe Paterno*

You will learn a lot about yourself if you stretch in the direction of goodness, of bigness, of kindness, of forgiveness, of emotional bravery.

- *Cheryl Strayed*

Women might be able to fake orgasms. But men can fake whole relationships.

- *Sharon Stone*

Equal rights for the sexes will be achieved only when mediocre women occupy high positions.

- *Françoise Giroud*

If your plan is for 1 year, plant rice; if your plan is for 10 years, plant trees; if your plan is for 100 years, educate children.

- *Confucius*

Life shrinks or expands in proportion to one's courage.

- *Anais Nin*

If you don't know where you are going, any road will do.

- *Neils Bohr*

Change the way you look at things, and the things you look at change.

- *Wayne Dyer*

The only people who accept change are toll takers.

- *Morris Cohen*

You can pay back the loan of gold but one lives forever in debt to those who are kind.

- *Paraphrase of a Malayan proverb*

Nothing endures but change.

- *Heraclides*

Always Remember:
True nobility isn't about
being better than
anyone else. It's about
being better than you
used to be.

- *Rumi*

Great ideas need landing gear as well as wings.

- *C.D. Jackson*

Good thoughts bear good fruit, bad thoughts bear bad fruit - and man is his own gardener.

- *James Allen*

A clear conscience is usually the sign of a bad memory.

- *Stephen Wright*

A man wrapped up in himself makes a very small package.

- *Benjamin Franklin*

Never argue with fools. They will lower you to their level, but then beat you with experience.

- *Unknown*

All that is needed for evil to succeed is that decent human beings do nothing.

- *Edmund Burke*

He who is not courageous enough to take risks will accomplish nothing in life.

- *Muhammad Ali*

"I can forgive but I cannot forget" is only another way of saying "I will not forgive." Forgiveness ought to be like a canceled note – torn in two and burned up so that it can never be shown against one.

- *Henry Ward Beecher*

I don't want to be a product of my environment. I want my environment to be a product of me.

- *Jack Nicholson (The Movie - The Departed)*

If the enemy is in range, so are you!

- *United States Army Infantry Manual*

Time is a versatile performer. It flies, marches on, heals all wounds, runs out and will tell.

- *Franklin P. Jones*

Go to heaven for the climate. Go to hell for the company.

- *Mark Twain*

Character is what you are. Reputation is what people think you are.

- *John Woode*

A government that robs Peter to pay Paul can always depend on the support of Paul.

- *George Bernard Shaw*

We are tomorrow's past.

- *Mary Web*

The budget should be balanced, the treasury should be refilled, public debt should be reduced, the arrogance of officialdom should be tempered and controlled, and the assistance to foreign lands should be curtailed lest Rome become bankrupt. People must again learn to work instead of living on public assistance.

- *Cicero*

Tact is for people who are not witty enough to be sarcastic.

- *Unknown*

Growing old isn't for sissies.

- *Dr. Marshall L. Cook*

Risk is the price you pay for opportunity.

- *A.J. Cooper (Character on TV Program - Las Vegas)*

Challenges don't build character; they reveal it.

- *Oppenheimer Fund TV Commercial*

Discourage litigation. Persuade your neighbors to compromise whenever you can. As a peacemaker the lawyer has a superior opportunity of being a good man. There will still be enough business.

- *Abraham Lincoln*

Good enough - isn't.

- *Jerry Baskin*

A wise man changes his mind. A fool never does.

- *Desmond Ford*

A winner is a dreamer who never gives up.

- *Nelson Mandela*

The reading of good books is like a conversation with the best men of past centuries.

- *Rene Descartes*

Your second life begins when you realize you have only one life.

- *Tom Hiddleston*

There is more to life than increasing its speed.

- *Mohandas K. Gandhi*

Forgiveness does not erase the past, but it does widen the future.

- *Paul Boese*

And what we students of history always learn is that the human being is a very complicated contraption and that they are not good or bad but are good and bad and the good comes out of the bad and the bad out of the good, and the devil take the hindmost.

- Robert Penn Warren

Keep Your Ego In Check - But Let Your Alter Ego Run Wild.

- *Don Rickles*

Some people try to turn back their odometers. Not me; I want people to know why I look this way. I have traveled a long way and some of the roads were not paved.

- *Will Rodgers*

The scariest moment is always just before you start.

- *Stephen King*

Have passion and
pride to be dynamic,
distinguished, and
extraordinary.

- *Mirna Lopez Freitag*

Everything should be made as simple as possible, but not simpler.

- *Albert Einstein*

It's worth remembering that it is often the small steps, not the giant leaps, that bring about the most lasting change.

- *Queen Elizabeth II*

Love is not a sprint; it's a marathon; a relentless pursuit that only ends when she falls in your arms or hits you with pepper spray.

- *Howard Wolowitz (Television show - The Big Bang Theory)*

Good soup and good character are both made at home.
-   *Herm Edwards*

If you don't have a celebration planned, you're not planning to celebrate.

-   *Nate Burleson*

People who love sausage and people who believe in justice should never watch either of them being made.

-   *Otto Von Bismarck*

The inherent vice of capitalism is the unequal sharing of the blessings. The inherent blessing of socialism is the equal sharing of the misery.

- *Winston Churchill*

Trip over love, you can get up. Fall in love, and you will fall forever.

- *Unknown*

For most of us the biggest stage we will ever play on is our funeral. For that we have virtually no say on the script, the direction, the production, the costuming, the setting, and so on. How fair is that?

- *Leon Kaatz*

No good deed goes unpunished!

- *Unknown*

If you find yourself in a hole, stop digging.

- *Will Rodgers*

You never get a second chance to make a first impression.

- *Unknown*

I fear the day that technology will surpass human interaction. The world will have a generation of idiots.

- *Albert Einstein*

Waste no time on anger, regret, or resentment, just get the job done.

- *Ruth Bater Ginsburg*

Justice may be blind but she has very sophisticated listening devices.

- *Edgar Argo*

Speak not against anyone whose burden you have not weighed yourself.

- *Marion Bradley*

It is never too late to give up our prejudices.

- *Henry David Thoreau*

The road to success is always under construction.

- *Lily Tomlin*

Your attitude will always determine your altitude.

- *Zig Ziglar*

Don't assume that paying the price for committing a crime ends when you walk out of jail. Rather, you should assume that every mistake you make in life can impact you for the rest of your life.

- *Leon Kaatz*

There are two gifts all parents should give their children: the first is roots; the second is wings.

- *Unknown*

Do not go where the path may lead. Go instead where there is no path and leave a trail.

- *Ralph Waldo Emerson*

Always go to other people's funerals. Otherwise, they won't come to yours.

- *Yogi Berra*

Censorship is telling a man he can't have a steak just because a baby can't chew it.

- *Mark Twain*

Life comes at you fast. If you turn away you might miss it.

- *Ferris Bueller*

If you let yourself think you can't do something you have taken the first step towards not being able to do it.

- *Leon Kaatz*

Perfection is not attainable, but if we chase perfection, we can catch excellence.

- *Vince Lombardi*

One of these days is none of these days.

- *English Proverb*

Raising A Child Is the Hardest Job I Ever Loved.

- *Stephanie Tsui*

There are a thousand thoughts lying within a man that he does not know till he takes up a pen to write.

- *William Makepeace Thackeray*

If you take too long to find your voice you run the risk of it being lost forever.

- *Leon Kaatz*

Generosity is not a quid pro quo. It should be its own reward.

- *Amy Dickinson*

Training is like fighting a gorilla. You don't stop when you are tired. You stop when the gorilla is tired.

- *Iggy Moore*

I really don't think life is about the I-could-have-beens. Life is only about the I-tried-to-do. I don't mind the failure, but I can't imagine that I'd forgive myself if I didn't try.

- *Nikki Giovanni*

God gives us children so death won't come as such a disappointment.

- *Evelyn Harper, Two and A Half Men*

If you fail to prepare - then prepare to fail.

- *Unknown*

The family is one of nature's masterpieces.

- *George Santayana*

Beauty comes in all ages, colors, shapes and forms. God never makes junk.

- *Kathy Ireland*

The only time you have too much fuel is when you are on fire.

- *Military Training Manual*

Being pushed out of your comfort zone doesn't mean you have to be uncomfortable. Embrace it. That is one way you grow and learn.

- *Leon Kaatz*

Too much of even a good thing is still too much.

- *Peter Bakker*

Like most people (so I assume) when I attend a funeral, I wonder what my own funeral will be like. If others have seen my life like I saw it there will be a lot of rejoicing; some from people celebrating what I accomplished and some from people happy to see me gone. That's probably the way it should be.

- *Leon Kaatz*

Into the well which supplies you with water, cast no stones.

- *The Talmud*

The cruelest lies are often told in silence.

- *Robert Louis Stevenson*

The reward of a thing well done is to have done it.

- *Ralph Waldo Emerson*

Every man has three names: one his father and mother gave him, one others call him, and one he acquires himself.

- *Unknown*

Age is merely the number of years the world has been enjoying you.

- *Unknown*

What we have to learn to do, we learn by doing.

- *Unknown*

Colors speak all languages.

- *Joseph Addison*

Thinking is like loving and dying. Each of us must do it for himself.

- *Josiah Royce*

Be slow in choosing a friend, slower in changing.

- *Ben Franklin*

The toughest thing about success is that you've got to keep on being a success.

- *Irving Berlin*

Open your mind and say, 'Ah'.

- *Unknown*

Someone is sitting in the shade today because someone planted a tree a long time ago.
- Warren Buffet

Those who lose today may win tomorrow...

- *Cervantes*

Dragons are too seldom.

- *Puppeteers from South Dakota*

There are defeats more triumphant than victories.

- *Montaigne*

I am a citizen of the world.

- *Diogenes*

Happy are those who can give without remembering and take without forgetting.

- *Unknown*

Tell me what you eat and I will tell you who you are.

- *Savarin*

A single rose can be my garden.

- *Unknown*

The best place to find a helping hand is at the end of your arm.

- *Unknown*

So many worlds, so much to do! So little done, such things to be.

- *Alfred Lord Tennyson*

It is by acts and not by ideas that people live.

- *Anatole France*

We like because we love despite.

- *Unknown*

Man was endowed with two ears and one tongue, that he may listen more than speak.

- *Zeno of Citium*

To teach is also to learn.

- *Japanese Proverb*

Half our life is spent trying to find something to do with the time we have rushed through life trying to save.

- *Will Rogers*

To leave is to die a little… one leaves behind a little of oneself at any hour, any place.

- *Edmond Haracourt*

A stranger is a friend you haven't met.

- *Unknown*

Although the world is full of suffering, it is also full of the overcoming of it.

- *Helen Keller*

Every definition is dangerous.

- *Erasmus*

Perseverance is the hard work you do after you get tired of doing the hard work you already did.

- *Newt Gingrich*

Conscience is the inner voice that warns us someone may be looking.

- *H.L. Mencken*

We protest against unjust criticism, but we accept unearned applause.

- *José Narosky*

One man with courage makes a majority.

- *Andrew Jackson*

He who praises everybody praises nobody.

- *Samuel Jackson*

Children are our most valuable resource.

- *Herbert Hoover*

Everyone is a moon and has a dark side which he never shows anybody.

- *Mark Twain*

What really matters is what happens in us, not to us.

- *Unknown*

Anybody can become angry—that is easy; but to be angry with the right person, and to the right degree, and at the right time, and for the right purpose, and in the right way - that is not within everybody's power and is not easy.

- *Aristotle*

Being virtuous is no feat once temptation ceases.

- *Danish proverb*

Laziness is nothing more than resting before you get tired.

- *Jules Renard*

Most of our so-called reasoning consists in finding arguments for going on believing as we already do.

- *James Harvey Robinson*

Don't push the river, it flows by itself.

- *F. Perls*

It is not a measure of a person's worth if God speaks to them. God speaks to all of us. The measure of a person's worth is who of us is listening.

- *Unknown*

Busy is a decision.

- *Debbie Millman*

It is difficult to see the picture when you are inside the frame.

- *R.S. Trapp*

Endings don't have to be failures, especially when you choose to end a project or shut down a business. Even the best gigs don't last forever. Nor should they.

- *Samin Nosrat*

A modest man is usually admired - if people ever hear of him.

- *Ed Howwe*

I firmly believe you never should spend your time being the former anything.

- *Condoleezza Rice*

It is fatal to know too much at the outset. Boredom comes as quickly to the traveler who knows his route as the novelist who is over-certain of his plot.

- *Paul Theroux*

Burnout is not the price you have to pay for success.

- *Arianna Huffington*

Money in a business is like gas in your car. You need to pay attention so you don't end up on the side of the road, but your trip is not a tour of gas stations.

- *Tim O'Reilly*

We do not remember days, we remember moments.

- *Unknown*

If at first the idea is not absurd, then there is no hope for it.

- *Albert Einstein*

It had long since come to my attention that people of accomplishment rarely sat back and let things happen to them. They went out and happened to things.

- *Leonardo Da Vinci*

Life is either a daring adventure or nothing at all.

- *Helen Keller*

Don't think being at the bottom of the totem pole is a bad thing…You have nowhere to go but up.

- *Dara Torres*

If you don't make mistakes, you're not working on hard enough problems. And that's a big mistake.

- *Frank Wilczek*

Lose an hour in the morning, chase it all day.

- *Yiddish saying*

Do not squander time, for that is the stuff life is made of.

- *Benjamin Franklin*

There is no way to happiness - happiness is the way.

- *Thich Nhat Hanh*

I prefer to be true to myself, even at the hazard of incurring the ridicule of others, rather than to be false, and to incur my own abhorrence.

- *Frederick Douglass*

Excellence is the next five minutes…Forget the long term. Make the next five minutes rock!

- *Tom Peters*

The simple willingness to improvise is more vital, in the long run, than research.

- *Rolf Potts*

Perfection is not when there is no more to add but no more to take away.

- *Antoine De Saint-Exupéry*

Love of bustle is not industry.

- *Seneca*

You can never leave footprints that last if you are always walking on tiptoe.

- *Leymah Gbowee*

Service to others is the rent you pay for your room here on earth.

- *Muhammad Ali*

Anything you build on a large scale or with intense passion invites chaos.

- *Francis Ford Coppola*

If you want a thing done well, do it yourself.

- Napoleon Bonaparte

There are many things of which a wise man might wish to be ignorant.

- *Ralph Waldo Emerson*

Love at first sight is easy to understand. It's when two people have been looking at each other for years that it becomes a miracle.

- *Sam Levenson*

Do not seek to follow in the footsteps of the wise, instead, seek what they sought.

- *Matsuo Bashō*

Too often we enjoy the comfort of opinion without the discomfort of thought.

- *John F. Kennedy*

Whoever thinks marriage is a 50-50 proposition doesn't know half of it.

- *Franklin P. Jones*

Anything worth doing is worth doing slowly.

- *Mae West*

If you find yourself in a fair fight, you didn't plan your mission properly.

- *Colonel David Hackworth*

The actual consequences of your actions matter far more than your actions themselves.

- *Liv Boeree*

Almost all advice given to writers by supposed experts is wrong.

- *Brian Koppelman*

The most important thing a father can do for his children is to love their mother.

- *Theodore Herbert*

In theory there is no difference between theory and practice. But, in practice, there is.

- Jan L.A. van deSnepscheut

The main thing is to keep the main thing the main thing.

- *Sarah Elizabeth Lewis*

It will never get easier than right now to recklessly pursue your passion.

- *Tommy Vietor*

If you set your goals ridiculously high and it's a failure, you will fail above everyone else's success.

- *James Cameron*

No society in human history ever suffered because its people became too reasonable.

- *Sam Harris*

I wake up each day with the firm conviction that I am nowhere near my full potential. 'Greatness' is a verb.

- *Maurice Ashley*

Those who are determined to be 'offended' will discover a provocation somewhere. We cannot possibly adjust enough to please the fanatics, and it is degrading to make the attempt.

- *Christopher Hitchens*

Those who are easily shocked should be shocked more often.

- *Mae West*

To dare is to lose one's footing momentarily. Not to dare is to lose oneself.

- *Søren Kierkegaard*

The key to a great life is simply having a bunch of great days. So, you can think about it one day at a time.

- *Mr. Money Mustache*

Do what you can, with what you have, where you are.

- *Theodore Roosevelt*

Originality only happens on the edges of reality.

- *Darren Aronofsky*

You can do so much in ten minutes' time. Ten minutes, once gone, are gone for good. Divide your life into ten-minute units and sacrifice as few of them as possible in meaningless activity.

- *Ingvar Kamprad*

Some of the most successful deals are those you don't do.

- *Evan Williams*

Don't spend time chasing a right answer or a right path, but instead spend time defining how you are going to approach whatever path you choose.

- *Laura R. Walker*

To be prepared against surprise is to be trained. To be prepared for surprise is to be educated.

- *James P. Carse*

In the end, winning is sleeping better.

- *Timothy Ferriss*

Make the most of yourself by fanning the tiny, inner sparks of possibility into flames of achievement.

- *Golda Meir*

It is no measure of health to be well adjusted to a profoundly sick society.

- *J. Krishnamurti*

Show up in every moment like you're meant to be there, because your energy precedes anything you could possibly say.

Marie Forleo

I'm not the strongest. I'm not the fastest. But I'm really good at suffering.

- *Amelia Boone*

When you stop caring about being right in the eyes of everyone…it's amazing how little you care to waste energy trying to convince people of your view.

- *Peter Attia*

When I let go of what I am, I become what I might be.

- *Lao Tzu*

The rule is: The basics are the basics, and you can't beat the basics.

- *Charles Poliquin*

All good things are wild and free.

- *Henry David Thoreau*

It is likely that most of what you currently learn at school will be irrelevant by the time you are 40… My best advice is to focus on personal resilience and emotional intelligence.

- *Yuval Noah Harari*

Great opportunities never have 'great opportunity' in the subject line.

- *Scott Belsky*

It is amazing what you can accomplish if you do not care who gets the credit.

- *Harry Truman*

In a real sense, to grow in life, I must be a seeker of stress.
- *Jim Loehr*

I happen to be in a very tough business where there are no alibis. It is good or it is bad, and the thousand reasons that interfere with a book being as good as possible are no excuses if it is not…Taking refuge in domestic successes, being good to your broke friends, etc., is merely a form of quitting.

- *Ernest Hemingway*

Discipline equals freedom.

- *Jocko Willink*

Routine, in an intelligent man, is a sign of ambition.

- *W.H. Auden*

Poets do not 'fit' into society, not because a place is denied them but because they do not take their 'places' seriously. They openly see its roles as theatrical, its styles as poses, its clothing costumes, its rules conventional, its crises arranged, its conflicts performed, and its metaphysics ideological.

- *James P. Carse*

Be the silence that listens.

- *Tara Brach*

Show me a family of readers, and I will show you the people who move the world.

- *Napoleon Bonaparte*

Our brains, our fear, our sense of what's possible, and the reality of 'only' 24 hours in a day give us preconceived notions of what is humanly possible.

- *Robert Rodriguez*

Out on the edge you see all kinds of things you can't see from the center. Big, undreamed-of things - the people on the edge see them first.

- *Kurt Vonnegut*

Judge a man by his questions rather than his answers.

- *Pierre-Marc-Gaston*

What you put in your mouth is a stressor, and what you say - what comes out of your mouth is also a stressor.

- *Charles Poliquin*

No one is qualified to tell you how you experience the world.

- *Vlad Zamfir*

Giant leaps often start with small steps.

- *Queen Elizabeth II*

Dreams are lovely. But they are just dreams. Fleeting, ephemeral, pretty. But dreams do not come true just because you dream them. It's hard work that makes things happen. It's hard work that creates change.

- *Shonda Rhimes*

There are only four stories: a love story between two people, a love story between three people, the struggle for power, and the journey. Every single book that is in the bookstore deals with these four archetypes, these four themes.

- *Paulo Coelho*

She who makes mock of her mother is in danger of Hell's fire.

- *Jacqueline Chase*

If I only had a little humility, I'd be perfect.

- *Ted Turner*

Intelligence is quickness in seeing things as they are.

- *George Santayana*

One of the advantages of being young is that you don't let common sense get in the way of doing things everybody else knows are impossible.

- *Unknown*

It is a great imperfection to complain unceasingly of little things.

- *Saint François de Sales*

You know that children are growing up when they start asking questions that have answers.

- *John J. Plomp*

Mondays are the potholes in the road of life.

- *Tom Wilson*

The optimist proclaims that we live in the best of all possible worlds, and the pessimist fears that this is true.

- *James Branch Cabell*

You can't blend in when you were born to stand out.

- *R.J. Palacio*

I like life. It's something to do.

- *Ronnie Shakes*

My grandfather always said that living is like licking honey off a thorn.

- *Louis Adamic*

A good leader inspires people to have confidence in the leader; a great leader inspires people to have confidence in themselves.

- *Eleanor Roosevelt*

In spite of the cost of living, it's still popular.
-   *Laurence J. Peter*

Life isn't fair. It's just fairer than death, that's all.

-   *William Goldman*

We learn from experience that men never learn anything from experience.

-   *George Bernard Shaw*

From birth to age 18, a girl needs good parents, from 18 to 35 she needs good looks, from 35 to 55 she needs a good personality, and from 55 on she needs cash.

- *Sophie Tucker*

Death is just a distant rumor to the young.

- *Andy Rooney*

Reinhart was never his mother's favorite - and he was an only child.

- *Thomas Berger*

Time is a great teacher, but unfortunately it kills all its pupils.

- *Hector Brlioz*

Many a man owes his success to his first wife and his second wife to his success.

- *Jim Backus*

I get my exercise acting as a pallbearer to my friends who exercise.

- *Chauncey Depew*

Success is getting up just one more time than you fall down.

- *Oliver Goldsmith*

A lady is one who never shows her underwear unintentionally.

- *Lillian Day*

Women who seek to be equal with men lack ambition.

- *Timothy Leary*

The only way to keep your health is to eat what you don't want, drink what you don't like, and do what you'd rather not.

- *Mark Twain*

Real knowledge is to know the extent of one's ignorance.

- *Confucius*

The most common of all follies is to believe passionately in the palpably not true. It is the chief occupation of mankind.

- *H.L. Mencken*

Wife - A former sweetheart.

- *H.L. Mencken*

The measure of a man's real character is what he would do if he knew he never would be found out.

- *Thomas Macaulay*

Natives who beat drums to drive off evil spirits are objects of scorn to smart Americans who blow horns to break up traffic jams.

- *Mary Ellen Kelly*

The average person thinks he isn't.

- *Father Larry Lorenzoni*

Ignorance of ignorance is the greatest ignorance.

- *Laurence J. Peter*

The most wonderful thing about life is that you can always begin again. No matter what ups and downs you are handed in life today, you can always begin again tomorrow.

- *Raiza Mendoza*

Virtue has never been as respectable as money.

- *Mark Twain*

The pendulum of school reform swings between extremes of permissiveness and puritanical rule making, and tends to afflict generations alternating with the worst of both philosophies. But professional educators have an obligation to take a firmer stand against the absurdities of each fleeting era. It is in moderating the progressive and traditional extremes that the most promising answers may be found.

- *Fred Hechinger*

Nowadays the illiterates can read and write.

- *Alberto Moravia*

Most conversations are simply monologues delivered in the presence of witnesses.

- *Margaret Millar*

To read without reflecting is like eating without digesting.

- *Edmund Burke*

So far as I can remember, there is not one word in the Gospels in praise of intelligence.

- *Bertrand Russell*

My interest in Afghanistan, specifically in the lives of Afghan women, showed me that there are serious challenges in some parts of the world for women just to live safe lives. But I also think that in many parts of the world – and certainly in the United States – it's a wonderful time for women. When George was president, I looked at the statistics of girls versus boys in the United States and realized that boys needed some attention too. We had focused so much on girls, and girls had become more successful than many boys in school. We expected more from boys in a way, without giving them the sort of nurturing that we did girls. So it's important that, while we continue to support women at home and around the world, we pay attention to boys too.

- *Laura Bush*

Man can learn nothing unless he proceeds from the know to the unknown.

- *Claude Bernard*

A mistake is evidence that somebody has tried to accomplish something.

- *John E. Babcock*

The world's great men have not commonly been great scholars, nor its great scholars' great men.

- *Oliver Wendell Holmes*

If 50 million people say a foolish thing, it is still a foolish thing.

- Anatole France

This thing that we call "Failure" is not the falling down, but the staying down.

- *Mary Pickford*

It isn't the experience of today that drives men mad. It is the remorse for something that happened yesterday, and the dread of what tomorrow may disclose.

- *Robert Jones Burdette*

Everyone makes mistakes. It is what you do afterwards that counts.

- *Kristan Higgins*

Learn more, know less.

- *Neil Strauss*

Jumping at several small opportunities may get us there more quickly than waiting for one big one to come along.

- *Hugh Allen*

People say that what we're all seeking is a meaning for life. I don't think that's what we're really seeking. I think that what we're seeking is an experience of being alive.

- *Joseph Campbell*

If you wish to know what a man is, place him in authority.

- *Yugoslav proverb*

The brightest flashes in the world of thought are incomplete until they have been proved to have their counterparts in the world of fact.

- *John Tyndall*

It may be too late already, but it's not as much too late now as it will be later.

- *C.H. Weisert*

A teacher affects eternity; he can never tell where his influence stops.

- *Henry Adams*

Nothing is so fatiguing as the eternal hanging on of an uncompleted task.

- *William James*

A good heart is better than all the heads in the world.

- *Edward Bulwer Lytton*

Parenthood remains the greatest single preserve of the amateur.

- *Alvin Toffler*

- If children grew up according to early indications, we should have nothing but geniuses.
  - *Johann Wolfgang Von Goethe*

The principal mark of genius is not perfection but originality, the opening of new frontiers.
  - *Arthur Koestler*

If you can find a path with no obstacles, it probably doesn't lead anywhere.
  - *Frank A. Clark*

Each of us will have to make the choices that allow us to be the largest versions of ourselves.

- *Julia Alvarez*

School is not preparation for life, but school is life.

- *John Dewey*

School and education should not be confused; it is only school that can be made easy.

- *Unknown*

Fame is proof that people are gullible.

- *Ralph Waldo Emmerson*

I find television very educating. Every time somebody turns on the set, I go into the other room and read a book.

- *Groucho Marx*

We all live under the same sky, but we don't all have the same horizon.

- *Konrad Adenauer*

Deliver me from writers who say the way they live doesn't matter. I'm not sure a bad person can write a good book. If art doesn't make us better, then what on earth is it for.

- *Alice Walker*

Educate your children to self-control…and you have done much to abolish misery from their future lives and crimes from society.

- *Daniel Webster*

He that has one eye is a prince among those that have none.

- *Thomas Fuller*

People are lonely because they build walls instead of bridges.

- *Unknown*

Whatever liberates our spirit without giving us mastery over ourselves is destructive.

- *Goethe*

What isn't tried won't work.

- *Claude McDonald*

Having once decided to achieve a certain task, achieve it at all costs of tedium and distaste. The gain in self-confidence of having accomplished a tiresome labor is immense.

- *Arnold Bennet*

Living is a constant process of deciding what we are going to do.

- *Jose Ortega y Gasset*

We either make ourselves miserable or we make ourselves strong. The amount of work is the same.

- *Carlos Cartenada*

If they can make penicillin out of moldy bread, they can sure make something out of you.

- *Muhammed Ali*

To conquer without risk is to triumph without glory.

- *Pierre Corneille*

To speak ill of others is a dishonest way of praising ourselves.

- *Will and Ariel Durant*

My mother drew a distinction between achievement and success. She said that "achievement is the knowledge that you have studied and worked hard and done the best that is in you. Success is being praised by others, and that's nice, too, but not as important or satisfying. Always aim for achievement and forget about success.

- *Helen Hayes*

Do what you can, with what you have, where you are.

- *Theodore Roosevelt*

The universe is under no obligation to make sense to you.

- *Neil Degrasse Tyson*

The way to get things done is not to mind who gets the credit of doing them.

- *Benjamin Jowett*

Malice will always find bad motives for good actions. Shall we therefore never do good?

- *Thomas Jefferson*

He conquers who endures.

- *Persius*

The best fertilizer is the shadow of the gardener.

- *Spanish Proverb*

In giving advice, seek to help, not please, your friend.

- *Solon*

We always like those who admire us, but we do not always like those whom we admire.

- *La Rochefoucauld*

A good thing to remember, a better thing to do…be part of the construction gang not of the wrecking crew.

- *Peter Bakker*

Don't hire a dog, then bark yourself.

- *David Ogilvy*

When you come to the end of your rope, tie a knot in it and hang on.

- *Peter Bakker*

Education is learning what you didn't even know you didn't know.

- *Daniel J. Boorstin*

Advice when most needed is least heeded.

- *Unknown*

People who ask for our advice almost never take it. Yet we should never refuse to give it, upon request, for it often helps us to see our own way more clearly.

- *Brendan Francis*

No answer is also an answer.

- *German proverb*

Knowing what must be done does away with fear.

- *Rosa Parks*

In America, the young are always ready to give to those who are older the benefits of their inexperience.

- *Oscar Wilde*

A hero is no braver than an ordinary man – but he is braver five minutes longer.

- *Ralph Waldo Emerson*

Never explain. Your friends do not need it…and your enemies will not believe you anyway.

- *Elbert Hubbard*

Bureaucracy is the art of making the possible impossible.

- Javier Pascual Salcedo

Civility, manners, and common sense cannot be legislated; they can only be bred.

- *Leon Kaatz*

We cannot create observers by saying "observe." But by giving them the power and the means for this observation, these means are processed through education of the senses.

- *Maria Montessori*

If a man does not keep pace with his companions, perhaps it is because he hears a different drummer. Let him step to the music which he hears, however measured   or far away.

- *Henry David Thoreau*

Keep cool; anger is not an argument.

- *Daniel Webster*

Anyone who keeps the ability to see beauty never grows old.

- *Franz Kafka*

Art is a higher type of knowledge than experience.

- *Aristotle*

No life is so hard that you can't make it easier by the way you take it.
- *Ellen Glasgow*

Whether you think you can or think you can't, you're right.

- *Henry Ford*

Acceptance of what has happened is the first step to overcoming the consequences of any misfortune.

- *William James*

The most difficult thing is the decision to act, the rest is merely tenacity.

- *Amelia Earhart*

A book is like a garden carried in the pocket.

- *Chinese proverb*

To acquire the habit of reading is to construct for yourself a refuge from almost all the miseries of life.

- *W. Somerset Maugham*

Most of us are willing to change, not because we see the light, but because we feel the heat.

- *Unknown*

If you behave in a dignified way you won't have to worry about your integrity because dignity is the manifestation of integrity.

- *Amy Dickinson*

Oh, what a tangled web we weave when at first, we do deceive.

- *Sir Walter Scott*

Sometimes the best way to convince someone he is wrong is to let him have his way.

- *Red O'Donnell*

Do not remove a fly from your friend's forehead with a hatchet.

- *Chinese proverb*

Civilization is a race between education and catastrophe.

- *H.G. Wells*

I wondered why so many old people read the bible. Then it dawned on me. They are cramming for the final exam.

- *George Carlin*

You may not control all the events that happen to you, but you can decide not to be reduced by them.

- *Maya Angelou*

Courage is not freedom from fear; it is being afraid and going on.

- *Unknown*

Curiosity may have killed the cat, but lack of curiosity would have killed thousands.

- *James Morrow*

Nothing is interesting, if you are not interested.

- *Helen MacInness*

You have your whole future ahead of you. Perfection doesn't happen right away.

- *Haruki Murakami*

Don't be discouraged in your journey if people talk badly about you, if people say you can't achieve something, don't let it discourage you; let it drive you forward. Listen to yourself, listen to your gut, and listen to the people in your life that you trust. Let your passions be your guide.

- *Alex Morgan*

And now we welcome the new year, full of things that have never been.

- *Rainer Maria Rilke*

The three hardest tasks in the world are neither physical feats nor intellectual achievements, but moral acts: to return love for hate to include the excluded, and to say, "I was wrong."

- *Sydney J. Harris*

The whole art of teaching is only the art of awakening the natural curiosity of young minds for the purpose of satisfying it afterwards.

- *Anatole France*

Bringing the student's world into the classroom is the most relevant act a teacher can perform.

- *Marc Robert*

We must not only give what we have; we must also give what we are.

- *Cardinal Joseph Mercier*

Don't be afraid to take a big step when one is indicated. You can't cross a chasm in two small jumps.

- *David Lloyd George*

If we are ever in doubt about what to do, it is a good rule to ask ourselves what we wish on the morrow that we had done.

- *John Lubbock*

It does not take much strength to do things, but it requires great strength to decide on what to do.

- *Elbert Hubbard*

The test of democracy is freedom of criticism.

- *David Ben-Gurion*

The "good" child may be frightened, and insecure, wanting only to please his parents by submitting to their will, while the "bad" child may have a will of his own and genuine interests but ones which do not please the parents.

- *Erich Fromm*

Beware of the man who won't be bothered with details.

- *William Feather*

Resolve to be tender with the young, compassionate with the aged, sympathetic with the striving and tolerant of the weak and wrong. Sometime in life you will have been all of these.

- *George Washington Carver*

Discipline of the school should proceed from the life of the school as a whole and not directly from the teacher.

- *John Dewey*

An educated man is one who can entertain a new idea, entertain another person, and entertain himself.

- *Sydney Herbert Wood*

Conscience is the inner voice that warns us that someone may be looking.

- *H.L. Mencken*

The difficult we do immediately. The impossible takes a little longer.

- *Slogan of the U.S.Army Corp of Engineers*

People sometimes make the mistake of confusing change with progress.

- *Jason Maur*

Good players want to be coached. Great players want to hear the truth.

- *Doc Rivers*

For most of history, Anonymous was a woman.

- *Virginia Woolf*

When you get into a tight place and everything goes against you, till it seems you could not hold on a minute longer, never give up then for that is just the place and time that the tide will turn.

- *Harriet Beecher Stowe*

I now perceive one immense omission in my psychology – the deepest principle of human nature is the craving to be appreciated.

- *William James*

Taking an interest in what students are thinking and doing is often a much more powerful form of encouragement than praise.

- *Robert Martin*

Divorce lawyers: God's way of telling you to stay single.

- *Lenny Briscoe (TV's Law and Order)*

When politicians complain that TV turns their proceedings into a circus it should be made plain that the circus was already there, and that TV has merely demonstrated that not all of the performers are well trained.

- *Edward R. Murrow*

Statistics should be used like a drunk uses a lamp post. Something to lean on but not for illumination.

- *Unknown*

There will come a time when you believe everything is finished. That will be the beginning.

- *Louis L'Amour*

Enthusiasm is contagious – and so is the lack of it.

- *Dale Carnegie*

He is well onward in the way of wisdom who can bear a reproof and mend by it.

- *Proverb*

Look for the good things, not the faults. It takes a good deal bigger-sized brain to find out what is not wrong with people and things, than to find out what is wrong.

- *R. L. Sharpe*

Revenge is a dish best served cold.

- *Eugène Sue*

It is difficult to inspire others to accomplish what you haven't been willing to try.

- *Confucius*

If you really want to do something, you'll find a way. If you don't, you'll find an excuse.

- *Jim Rohn*

It is because of our unassailable enthusiasm, our profound reverence for education, that we habitually demand of it the impossible. The teacher is expected to perform a choice and varied series of miracles.

- *Agnes Repplier*

Be obscure clearly.

- *E. B. White*

Never give an excuse that you would not be willing to accept.

- *Unknown*

You must be the change you wish to see in the world.

- Mahatma Gandhi

You'll find in no park or city, A monument to a committee.

- *Victoria Pasternak*

Even in the kindest and gentlest of schools, children are afraid, many of them a great deal of the time, some of them almost all of the time. This is a hard fact to deal with. What can we do about it?

- *John Holt*

The prime purpose of eloquence is to keep other people from speaking.

- *Louis Vermeil*

Learning is not child's play; we cannot learn without pain.
- *Aristotle*

I cannot give you the formula for success, but I can give you the formula for failure – which is: Try to please everybody.

- *Abraham Lincoln*

Many great things indeed have been achieved by those who chose not to leap into the mainstream.

- *Joan Mondale*

I had to make my own living and my own opportunity. But I made it! Don't sit down and wait for opportunities to come. Get up and make them.

- *Madam CJ Walker*

When a true genius appears in the world, you may know him by this sign that the dunces are all in the confederacy against him.

- *Jonathan Swift*

Some pursue happiness – others create it.

- *Helen Keller*

Always remember others may hate you, but those who hate you don't win unless you hate them.

- *Richard Nixon*

Commandment Number One of any truly civilized society is this: Let people be different.

- *David Grayson*

Any Ship Can Be a Minesweeper - Once!

- *U.S. Navy Training Manual*

The best preparation for being a happy and useful man or woman is to live fully as a child.

- *Plowden Report*

How glorious it is, and also how painful it is, to be an exception.

- *Alfred de Musset*

The only thing we learn from history is that we do not learn.

- *Earl Warren*

There are no degrees of honesty.

- *Ronald Reagan*

The finest thought runs the risk of being irretrievably forgotten if it is not written down.

- *Arthur Schopenhauer*

To the optimist - the glass is half full. To the pessimist - the glass is half empty. To the engineer - the glass is twice as big as it needs to be.

- *Unknown*

There comes a time when you should stop expecting other people to make a big deal about your birthday; that time is age 11.

- *Dave Barry*

A person who is nice to you, but rude to the waiter, is not a nice person.

- *Dave Barry*

Success doesn't come without education and hard work.

- *Sandy Martinez*

Impatience is waiting in a hurry.

- *Unknown*

The shoe that fits one person pinches another: there is no recipe for living that suits all cases.

- *Carl Jung*

Wise men learn more from fools than fools from wise men.

- *Cato*

Probably no man ever had a friend that he did not dislike a little.

- *E. W. Howe*

There are no easy methods of learning difficult things: the method is to close your door: give out that you are not home, and work.

- *Joseph de Maistre*

If there is no wind, row.

- *Latin proverb*

Courage isn't having the strength to go on - it is going on when you don't have strength.

- *Napoleon Bonaparte*

What is more wonderful than the delight which the mind feels when it knows? This delight is not for anything beyond knowing, but it is in the act of knowing it. It is the satisfaction of a primary instinct.

- *Mark Rutherford*

Some people will never learn anything, for this reason: because they understand everything too soon.

- *Alexander Pope*

A library is a hospital for the mind.

- *Alvin Toffler*

The trouble with facts is that there are so many of them.

- *Samuel Crothers*

Children need love, especially when they do not deserve it.

- *Harold Hulbert*

Love is saying "I feel differently" instead of "You're wrong."

- *Unknown*

Elegance is not about being noticed, it's about being remembered.

- *Giorgio Armani*

Be grateful for luck, but don't depend on it.

- *William Feather*

Rudeness is a weak man's imitation of strength.

- *Eric Hoffer*

If you want to see what children can do, you must stop giving them things.

- *Norman Douglas*

Only when children have had time to play and explore new materials in their own way will they be able to see the materials as learning materials.

- *Mary Baratta-Lorton*

One may go a long way after one is tired.

- *French proverb*

Few things are harder to put up with than the annoyance of a good example.

- *Samuel Langhorne Clemens*

We strain hardest for things which are almost, but not quite, within our reach.

- *Frederick Faber*

An inability to stay quiet is one of the most conspicuous failings of mankind.

- *Walter Bagehot*

Somehow, if you really attend to the real, it tells you everything.

- *Robert Pollock*

Don't tell me how hard you work. Tell me how much you get done.

- *James Lang*

We read every day, with astonishment, things which we see every day without surprise.

- *Lord Chesterfield*

We cannot create an observer by saying "observe," but by giving them the power and the means for this observation, and these means are procured through education of the senses.

- *Maria Montessori*

Every man has a right to his opinion, but no man has a right to be wrong in his facts.

- *Bernard Baruch*

Politics is for the present; an equation is forever.

- *Albert Einstein*

Hello, fear. Thank you for being here. You're my indication that I'm doing what I need to do.

- *Cheryl Strayed*

A woman's work is never done.

- *Unknown*

It's easier to critique than it is to create.

- Unknown

Laugh and you will live without Medicare until you are 100.

- *Julie Newar*

Among the smaller duties of life, I hardly know anyone more important than that of not praising where praise is not due.

- *Sydney Smith*

A diplomat is a man who always remembers his wife's birthday but never remembers her age.

- *Robert Frost*

Seize from every moment its unique novelty, and do not prepare your joys.

- *André Gide*

Who Am I??? I am more deadly than the screaming shells from the howitzer. I win without killing. I tear down homes, break hearts, and wreck lives. I travel on the wings of the wind. No innocence is strong enough to intimidate me, no purity pure enough to daunt me. I have no regard for truth, no respect for justice, no mercy for the defenseless... My victims are as numerous as the sands of the sea, and often as innocent. I never forget and seldom forgive. My name is Gossip.

- *Morgan Blake*

Fitting in is overrated. I spent my first few years at my first job out of college doing everything I could to make myself more like the people around me. It didn't bring out the best in me - and it didn't position me to bring out the best in others. The best advice I have to offer is: Seek out people and environments that empower you to be nothing but yourself.

- *Melinda Gates*

Musicians don't retire; they stop when there's no more music in them.

- *Louis Armstrong*

The greater a man is, the more distasteful is praise and flattery to him.

- *John Burroughs*

It is never too late to give up our prejudices.

- *Henry David Thoreau*

Headmasters have powers at their disposal with which Prime Ministers have never yet been invested.

- *Winston Churchill*

Procrastination is the father of failure.

- *Elbert Hubbard*

The way a book is read – which is to say, the qualities a reader brings to a book- can have as much to do with its worth as anything the author puts into it.

- *Norman Cousins*

Life will reward you,
but not always by
the route you expect.

- *Edna Rodriguez*

No noble thing can be done without risks.

- *Montaigne*

One of the reasons mature people stop learning is that they become less and less willing to risk failure.

- *John Gardner*

A person who does not read has no advantage over a person who cannot read.

- *Unknown*

The school is the last expenditure upon which America should be willing to economize.

- *Franklin D. Roosevelt*

There is no such thing as a great talent without great willpower.

- *Honore de Balzac*

If I despised myself, it would be no compensation if everyone saluted me, and if I respect myself, it does not trouble me if others hold me lightly.

- *Max Nordau*

The ultimate result of shielding men from folly is to fill the world with fools.

- *Herbert Spencer*

I can give you a six-word formula for success. Think things through – then follow through.

- *Eddie Rickenbacker*

Success is not a magic ingredient that can be supplied by teachers. Building on strengths allows students to create their own success.

- *Robert Martin*

We are so accustomed to wearing a disguise before others that eventually we are unable to recognize ourselves.

- *La Rochefoucauld*

The common idea that success spoils people by making them vain, egotistic, and self-complacent is erroneous; on the contrary, it makes them, for the most part, humble, tolerant, and kind. Failure makes people cruel and bitter.

- *W. Somerset Maugham*

There's nothing wrong with teenagers that reasoning with them won't aggravate.

- *Unknown*

The main problem with teenagers is that they're just like their parents were at their age.

- *Unknown*

Have a vision of excellence, a dream of success, and work like hell.

- Dr. Samuel DuBois Cook

There is only one success- to be able to spend your life in your own way.

- *Christopher Morley*

Everyone has talent; what is rare is the courage to follow the talent to the dark place where it leads.

- *Erica Jong*

Our chief want in life is somebody who will make us do what we can.

- *Ralph Waldo Emerson*

Everything should be made as simple as possible, but not one bit simpler.

- *Albert Einstein*

One might as well say he has sold when no one had bought as to say he has taught when no one has learned.

- *John Dewey*

People sometimes say, "I would like to teach if only pupils cared to learn." But then there would be little need of teaching.

- *George Herbert Palmer*

You can't do a kindness too soon…because you never know how soon… it will be too late.

- *Ralph Waldo Emerson*

Teaching youngsters isn't much like making steel…and as essential as good technique is, I don't think education is basically a technological problem. It is a problem of drawing out of each youngster the best he has to give and helping him to see the world he is involved in clearly enough to become himself-among other people-in it, while teaching him the skills he will need in the process.

- *Edgar Friedenberg*

Every man prefers belief to the exercise of judgment.

- *Seneca*

Always be shorter than anybody dared hope.

- *Lord Reading*

Every man…should periodically be compelled to listen to opinions which are infuriating to him. To hear nothing but what is pleasing to one is to make a pillow of the mind.

- *John Ervine*

Character is power.

- *Booker T. Washington*

What would be the use of immortality to a person who cannot use well half an hour?'

- *Ralph Waldo Emerson*

Drag your thoughts away from your troubles-by the ears, by the heels, or any other way, so you can manage it; it's the healthiest thing a body can do.

- *Mark Twain*

Life is a series of experiences, each one of which makes us bigger, even though sometimes it is hard to realize this.

- *Henry Ford*

The chief lesson I have learned in a long life is that the only way to make a man trustworthy is to trust him; and the surest way to make him untrustworthy is to distrust him and show your distrust.

- *Henry L. Stimson*

He is a fool that cannot conceal his wisdom.

- *Benjamin Franklin*

Children who are treated as if they are uneducable almost invariably become uneducable.

- *Kenneth Clark*

At the end of the day, we can endure much more than we think we can.

- *Frida Kahlo*

You may be deceived if you trust too much, but you will live in torment if you do not trust enough.

- *Frank Crane*

The difference between the right word and the almost right word is the difference between lightning and the lightning bug.

- *Mark Twain*

For me, the big chore is always the same – how to begin a sentence, how to continue it, how to complete it.

- *Claude Simon*

Equal opportunity. To be judged on merit. The change is not just how women are regarded by men, but how women regard themselves. You know, it starts with you.

- *Sylvia Earle*

Though we travel the world over to find the beautiful, we must carry it with us or we find it not.

- *Ralph Waldo Emerson*

Remember tonight, for it is the beginning of always.

- *Dante Alighieri*

You don't practice something until you get it right. You practice it until you can't get it wrong.

- *Geno Auriemma*

You only have what you give. It's by spending yourself that you become rich.

- *Isabel Allende*

I belong to myself.

- *Alicia Garcia*

Real change, enduring change, happens one step at a time.

- *Ruth Bater Ginsburg*

The Authors

Adam Chase Laningham, M.Ed
Author, Consultant, Educator, &
Owner, www.BrightChildAZ.com

Adam Laningham, author of Gifted Children & How Trauma Impacts Them, and Thinkology 2.0, has over 20 years of experience in the field of education. Adam was recognized as the 2014 Arizona Gifted Teacher of the Year, he has taught at several schools in multiple grade levels, created and facilitated numerous gifted programs, and also served as a district gifted services manager coordinating programs for over 6000 gifted students.

Adam has served on the Board of Directors for the Arizona Association for Gifted & Talented for many years and is currently the President Elect of SENG (Supporting the Emotional Needs of the Gifted). He is an Advisor for CogAT Riverside Insights and a founding member of Callisto (supporting gifted foster youth). As founder and owner of Bright Child AZ, Adam is an international speaker, consultant, and gifted advocate. His company offers, consulting, training, books & resources, enrichment courses, advocacy and much more..

Bright Child AZ

PROFESSIONALLY CURATED RESOURCES
FOR CURIOUS LEARNERS

Nathan Levy
Author, Consultant, & President of
Nathan Levy Books, LLC
www.StorieswithHoles.com

Nathan Levy is a dynamic educator, author and speaker. He has been a successful teacher, principal, gifted coordinator and supervisor of instruction in urban, suburban and rural school districts. In his role as consultant, Nathan continues to be a hands-on demonstrator of effective techniques for gifted, special education, and regular education children. Mr. Levy currently tours internationally sharing his expertise and knowledge. He has written more than sixty books that are used in thousands of classrooms and homes on five continents.

His books include: Beyond Schoolwork, Write from the Beginning, There Are Those, the Whose Clues, Intriguing Questions, and the famous Stories With Holes series. His newest books, Teachers' Guide to Trauma, Brain Whys, and Resiliency Through the Arts are being well received by educators and parents.

Nathan Levy is in high demand as a consultant to private and public schools in the areas of critical/creative thinking, writing, science/math teaching, differentiation, gifted, hard to reach learners and leadership. Nathan Levy is Past President of the New Jersey Association of Gifted Children.

Peter M. Bakker is a retired insurance executive living with his wife, Peggy, in a self-restored 1800 tavern in Barkhamsted, CT. He and his wife have been active in many community organizations over the past 50 years. Peter's father, a Dutch immigrant, was the inspiration for Peter's lifelong interest in quotes.

Leon Kaatz is a semi-retired lawyer living in Salem, CT. He has a bachelor's degree in mathematics from MIT and spent the first 10 years of his adult life working in math and science. He started collecting quotes in the 1990's when the *Hartford Courant* printed a thought of the day on the comics page. If they hadn't printed it on the comics page or the sports page, he might never have gotten started.

More Resources

Bright Child AZ

**PROFESSIONALLY CURATED RESOURCES
FOR CURIOUS LEARNERS**

Workshops and Professional Development

Bright Child AZ supports children, parents, and educators. We specialize in gifted education, twice-exceptionalism, creativity, social, and emotional support. Our team of professionals loves supporting our parents and educators, topic specialties consist of supporting twice-exceptional learners, gifted learners, using gifted strategies to support all learners, proven strategies to use in the classroom, parenting support and more. We build workshops and professional development to meet the needs of our clients all around the country. Please visit our website for more topics and services or email us for specific needs.

Please let us know how we can support you!

Adam@brightchildbooks.com

Bright Child AZ

PROFESSIONALLY CURATED RESOURCES
FOR CURIOUS LEARNERS

Some of our *Professionally Curated Resources* are:

- Gifted Children and How Trauma Impacts Them
- Gifted & Struggling - Twice-Exceptional Children Series
- Thinking and Writing Activities for the Brain! Book 1 & 2
- Quotes to Make you Brilliant & Quotes to Keep You Brilliant
- Thinkology 2.0 Gifted Edition (Digital Version)
- Intriguing Questions (Digital Version)
- Teachers' Guide to Resiliency Through the Arts
- Brain Whys?
- All Nathan Levy, Free Spirit, and Penguin Random House books
- *And much more!*

More resources are being added all the time. Please let us know if you can help you find the tools you need to engage and support your children!
Adam@brightchildbooks.com

www.StoriesWithHoles.com

Workshops and Professional Development

At Stories With Holes, we are committed to fostering lifelong learning by providing resources and professional development opportunities to children and adults alike. Our expert team, led by International Speaker, Author, and accomplished Gifted Educator, Nathan Levy, can tailor make presentations that directly fit the needs of your school, business, or organization. Our hands on, interactive workshops offer the perfect setting to gain access to practical strategies that meet the needs of our gifted children as well as those from across all learning spectrums.

To book a dynamic workshop tailored to your needs, please call 732-605-1643 or email us at nlevy103@comcast.net.

www.StoriesWithHoles.com

Books and Resources

Some of our select resources are:

- Beyond Schoolwork
- Nathan Levy's A.C.T.1
- Teachers' Guide to Trauma
- Quotes to Make you Brilliant & Quotes to Keep You Brilliant
- Trauma Informed Teaching Strategies That Are Good for All
- School Leaders' Guide to Trauma Sensitive Schools
- Nathan Levy's Test Booklet
- Creativity Day by Day
- Write, From the Beginning Revised Edition

Book Series:

- Stories with Holes
- Intriguing Questions
- Whose Clues

For more information or help in selecting resources, please call 732-605-1643 or email us at nlevy103@comcast.net.

Made in the USA
Las Vegas, NV
19 January 2024